Michael J Paine '59

PROUST

D1270187

PROUST

By

SAMUEL BECKETT

' E fango è il mondo '
LEOPARDI

GROVE PRESS   **NEW YORK**

ALL RIGHTS RESERVED
FIRST PUBLISHED
1931

Library of Congress Catalog Card No. 57-5313

Proust is published in three editions:
An Evergreen Book (E-50)
A hard bound edition
A specially bound, Limited Edition of 250 numbered copies,
signed by the author

Grove Press Books and Evergreen Books
are published by Barney Rosset
795 Broadway   *New York, N. Y.*

MANUFACTURED IN THE UNITED STATES OF AMERICA

FOREWORD

THERE is no allusion in this book to the
legendary life and death of Marcel Proust, nor
to the garrulous old dowager of the Letters,
nor to the poet, nor to the author of the
Essays, nor to the Eau de Selzian correlative
of Carlyle's 'beautiful bottle of soda-water.'
I have preferred to retain the titles in French.
The translations of text are my own.   The re-
ferences are to the abominable edition of the
Nouvelle Revue Française, in sixteen volumes.

PROUST

THE Proustian equation is never simple. The
unknown, choosing its weapons from a hoard
of values, is also the unknowable. And the
quality of its action falls under two signatures. In
Proust each spear may be a spear of Telephus. This
dualism in multiplicity will be examined more closely
in relation to Proust's ' perspectivism.' For the pur-
poses of this synthesis it is convenient to adopt the
inner chronology of the Proustian demonstration,
and to examine in the first place that double-headed
monster of damnation and salvation—Time.

The scaffolding of his structure is revealed to the
narrator in the library of the Princesse de Guermantes (one time Mme. Verdurin), and the nature
of its materials in the matinée that follows. His book
takes form in his mind. He is aware of the many
concessions required of the literary artist by the
shortcomings of the literary convention. As a
writer he is not altogether at liberty to detach effect
from cause. It will be necessary, for example, to
interrupt (disfigure) the luminous projection of subject desire with the comic relief of features. It will
be impossible to prepare the hundreds of masks that

rightly belong to the objects of even his most dis-interested scrutiny. He accepts regretfully the sacred ruler and compass of literary geometry. But he will refuse to extend his submission to spatial scales, he will refuse to measure the length and weight of man in terms of his body instead of in terms of his years. In the closing words of his book he states his position : ' But were I granted time to accomplish my work, I would not fail to stamp it with the seal of that Time, now so forcibly present to my mind, and in it I would describe men, even at the risk of giving them the appearance of mon-strous beings, as occupying in Time a much greater place than that so sparingly conceded to them in Space, a place indeed extended beyond measure, because, like giants plunged in the years, they touch at once those periods of their lives—separated by so many days—so far apart in Time.'

Proust's creatures, then, are victims of this pre-dominating condition and circumstance—Time ; victims as lower organisms, conscious only of two dimensions and suddenly confronted with the mys-tery of height, are victims : victims and prisoners. There is no escape from the hours and the days. Neither from to-morrow nor from yesterday. There is no escape from yesterday because yesterday has deformed us, or been deformed by us. The mood is of no importance. Deformation has taken place.

Yesterday is not a milestone that has been passed, but a daystone on the beaten track of the years, and irremediably part of us, within us, heavy and dangerous. We are not merely more weary because of yesterday, we are other, no longer what we were before the calamity of yesterday. A calamitous day, but calamitous not necessarily in content. The good or evil disposition of the object has neither reality nor significance. The immediate joys and sorrows of the body and the intelligence are so many superfoetations. Such as it was, it has been assimilated to the only world that has reality and significance, the world of our own latent consciousness, and its cosmography has suffered a dislocation. So that we are rather in the position of Tantalus, with this difference, that we allow ourselves to be tantalised. And possibly the perpetuum mobile of our disillusions is subject to more variety. The aspirations of yesterday were valid for yesterday's ego, not for to-day's. We are disappointed at the nullity of what we are pleased to call attainment. But what is attainment? The identification of the subject with the object of his desire. The subject has died— and perhaps many times—on the way. For subject B to be disappointed by the banality of an object chosen by subject A is as illogical as to expect one's hunger to be dissipated by the spectacle of Uncle eating his dinner. Even suppose that by one of those

3

rare miracles of coincidence, when the calendar of facts runs parallel to the calendar of feelings, realisation takes place, that the object of desire (in the strictest sense of that malady) is achieved by the subject, then the congruence is so perfect, the time-state of attainment eliminates so accurately the time-state of aspiration, that the actual seems the inevitable, and, all conscious intellectual effort to reconstitute the invisible and unthinkable as a reality being fruitless, we are incapable of appreciating our joy by comparing it with our sorrow. Voluntary memory (Proust repeats it ad nauseam) is of no value as an instrument of evocation, and provides an image as far removed from the real as the myth of our imagination or the caricature furnished by direct perception. There is only one real impression and one adequate mode of evocation. Over neither have we the least control. That reality and that mode will be discussed in their proper place.

But the poisonous ingenuity of Time in the science of affliction is not limited to its action on the subject, that action, as has been shown, resulting in an unceasing modification of his personality, whose permanent reality, if any, can only be apprehended as a retrospective hypothesis. The individual is the seat of a constant process of decantation, decantation from the vessel containing the fluid of future time, sluggish, pale and monochrome, to the vessel containing the

4

fluid of past time, agitated and multicoloured by the phenomena of its hours. Generally speaking, the former is innocuous, amorphous, without character, without any Borgian virtue. Lazily considered in anticipation and in the haze of our smug will to live, of our pernicious and incurable optimism, it seems exempt from the bitterness of fatality : in store for us, not in store in us. On occasions, however, it is capable of supplementing the labours of its colleague. It is only necessary for its surface to be broken by a date, by any temporal specification allowing us to measure the days that separate us from a menace—or a promise. Swann, for example, contemplates with doleful resignation the months that he must spend away from Odette during the summer. One day Odette says : ' Forcheville (her lover, and, after the death of Swann, her husband) is going to Egypt at Pentecost.' Swann translates : ' I am going with Forcheville to Egypt at Pentecost.' The fluid of future time freezes, and poor Swann, face to face with the *future* reality of Odette and Forcheville in Egypt, suffers more grievously than even at the misery of his present condition. The narrator's desire to see La Berma in *Phèdre* is stimulated more violently by the announcement ' Doors closed at two o'clock ' than by the mystery of Bergotte's ' Jansenist pallor and solar myth.' His indifference at parting from Albertine at the end of the day in Balbec is

5

transformed into the most horrible anxiety by a simple remark addressed by her to her aunt or to a friend : ' To-morrow, then, at half-past eight.' The tacit understanding that the future can be controlled is destroyed. The future event cannot be focussed, its implications cannot be seized, until it is definitely situated and a date assigned to it. When Albertine was his prisoner, the possibility of her escape did not seriously disturb him, because it was indistinct and abstract, like the possibility of death. Whatever opinion we may be pleased to hold on the subject of death, we may be sure that it is meaningless and valueless. Death has not required us to keep a day free. The art of publicity has been revolutionised by a similar consideration. Thus I am exhorted, not merely to try the aperient of the Shepherd, but to try it at seven o'clock.

So far we have considered a mobile subject before an ideal object, immutable and incorruptible. But our vulgar perception is not concerned with other than vulgar phenomena. Exemption from intrinsic flux in a given object does not change the fact that it is the correlative of a subject that does not enjoy such immunity. The observer infects the observed with his own mobility. Moreover, when it is a case of human intercourse, we are faced by the problem of an object whose mobility is not merely a function of the subject's, but independent and personal : two

separate and immanent dynamisms related by no
system of synchronisation. So that whatever the
object, our thirst for possession is, by definition, in-
satiable. At the best, all that is realised in Time (all
Time produce), whether in Art or Life, can only be
possessed successively, by a series of partial annexa-
tions—and never integrally and at once. The tragedy
of the Marcel-Albertine liaison is the type-tragedy of
the human relationship whose failure is preordained.
My analysis of that central catastrophe will clarify
this too abstract and arbitrary statement of Proust's
pessimism. But for every tumour a scalpel and a
compress. Memory and Habit are attributes of the
Time cancer. They control the most simple Proustian episode, and an understanding of their mechan-
ism must precede any particular analysis of their
application. They are the flying buttresses of the
temple raised to commemorate the wisdom of the
architect that is also the wisdom of all the sages, from
Brahma to Leopardi, the wisdom that consists not in
the satisfaction but in the ablation of desire :

> ' In noi di cari inganni
> non che la speme, il desiderio è spento.'

* *

*

The laws of memory are subject to the more general
laws of habit. Habit is a compromise effected between the individual and his environment, or be-

7

tween the individual and his own organic eccentricities, the guarantee of a dull inviolability, the lightning-conductor of his existence. Habit is the ballast that chains the dog to his vomit. Breathing is habit. Life is habit. Or rather life is a succession of habits, since the individual is a succession of individuals; the world being a projection of the individual's consciousness (an objectivation of the individual's will, Schopenhauer would say), the pact must be continually renewed, the letter of safe-conduct brought up to date. The creation of the world did not take place once and for all time, but takes place every day. Habit then is the generic term for the countless treaties concluded between the countless subjects that constitute the individual and their countless correlative objects. The periods of transition that separate consecutive adaptations (because by no expedient of macabre transubstantiation can the grave-sheets serve as swaddling-clothes) represent the perilous zones in the life of the individual, dangerous, precarious, painful, mysterious and fertile, when for a moment the boredom of living is replaced by the suffering of being. (At this point, and with a heavy heart and for the satisfaction or disgruntlement of Gideans, semi and integral, I am inspired to concede a brief parenthesis to all the analogivorous, who are capable of interpreting the 'Live dangerously,' that victorious hiccough in vacuo, as the

8

national anthem of the true ego exiled in habit. The Gideans advocate a habit of living—and look for an epithet. A nonsensical bastard phrase. They imply a hierarchy of habits, as though it were valid to speak of good habits and bad habits. An automatic adjustment of the human organism to the conditions of its existence has as little moral significance as the casting of a clout when May is or is not out ; and the exhortation to cultivate a habit as little sense as an exhortation to cultivate a coryza.) The suffering of being : that is, the free play of every faculty. Because the pernicious devotion of habit paralyses our attention, drugs those handmaidens of perception whose co-operation is not absolutely essential. Habit is like Françoise, the immortal cook of the Proust household, who knows what has to be done, and will slave all day and all night rather than tolerate any redundant activity in the kitchen. But our current habit of living is as incapable of dealing with the mystery of a strange sky or a strange room, with any circumstance unforeseen in her curriculum, as Françoise of conceiving or realising the full horror of a Duval omelette. Then the atrophied faculties come to the rescue, and the maximum value of our being is restored. But less drastic circumstances may produce this tense and provisional lucidity in the nervous system. Habit may not be dead (or as good as dead, doomed to die) but sleeping. This second and more fugitive experience may or may not be exempt from pain. It does not inaugurate a period of transition. But the first and major mode is inseparable from suffering and anxiety—the suffering of the dying and the jealous anxiety of the ousted. The old ego dies hard. Such as it was, a minister of dulness, it was also an agent of security. When it ceases to perform that second function, when it is opposed by a pheno-menon that it cannot reduce to the condition of a comfortable and familiar concept, when, in a word, it betrays its trust as a screen to spare its victim the spectacle of reality, it disappears, and the victim, now an ex-victim, for a moment free, is exposed to that reality—an exposure that has its advantages and its disadvantages. It disappears—with wailing and gnashing of teeth. The mortal microcosm cannot forgive the relative immortality of the macrocosm. The whisky bears a grudge against the decanter. The narrator cannot sleep in a strange room, is tortured by a high ceiling, being used to a low ceiling. What is taking place? The old pact is out of date. It contained no clause treating of high ceilings. The habit of friendship for the low ceiling is ineffectual, must die in order that a habit of friendship for the high ceiling may be born. Between this death and that birth, reality, intolerable, absorbed feverishly by his consciousness at the extreme limit of its intensity, by his total consciousness organised to avert the disaster, to create the new habit that will empty the mystery of its threat—and also of its beauty. 'If Habit,' writes Proust, 'is a second nature, it keeps us in ignorance of the first, and is free of its cruelties and its enchantments.' Our first nature, therefore, corresponding, as we shall see later, to a deeper instinct than the mere animal instinct of self-preservation, is laid bare during these periods of abandonment. And its cruelties and enchantments are the cruelties and enchantments of reality. 'Enchantments of reality' has the air of a paradox. But when the object is perceived as particular and unique and not merely the member of a family, when it appears independent of any general notion and detached from the sanity of a cause, isolated and inexplicable in the light of ignorance, then and then only may it be a source of enchantment. Unfortunately Habit has laid its veto on this form of perception, its action being precisely to hide the essence—the Idea—of the object in the haze of conception—preconception. Normally we are in the position of the tourist (the traditional specification would constitute a pleonasm), whose aesthetic experience consists in a series of identifications and for whom Baedeker is the end rather than the means. Deprived by nature of the faculty of cognition and by upbringing of any acquaintance with the laws of dynamics, a brief inscription immortalises his emotion. The creature of habit turns aside from the object that cannot be made to correspond with one or other of his intellectual prejudices, that resists the propositions of his team of syntheses, organised by Habit on labour-saving principles.

Examples of these two modes—the death of Habit and the brief suspension of its vigilance—abound in Proust. I will transcribe two incidents in the life of the narrator. Of these the first, illustrative of the pact renewed, is extremely important as preparing a later incident that I will have occasion to discuss in relation to Proustian memory and Proustian revelation. The second exemplifies the pact waived in the interests of the narrator's via dolorosa.

The narrator arrives at Balbec-Plage, a holiday resort in Normandy, for the first time, accompanied by his grandmother. They are staying at the Grand Hotel. He enters his room, feverish and exhausted after his journey. But sleep, in this inferno of unfamiliar objects, is out of the question. All his faculties are on the alert, on the defensive, vigilant and taut, and as painfully incapable of relaxation as the tortured body of La Balue in his cage, where he could neither stand upright nor sit down. There is no room for his body in this vast and hideous apartment, because his attention has peopled it with gigantic furniture, a storm of sound and an agony of colour. Habit has not had time to silence the explosions of the clock, reduce the hostility of the violet curtains, remove the furniture and lower the inaccessible vault of this belvedere. Alone in this room that is not yet a room but a cavern of wild beasts, invested on all sides by the implacable strangers whose privacy he has disturbed, he desires to die. His grandmother comes in, comforts him, checks the stooping gesture that he makes to unbutton his boots, insists on helping him to undress, puts him to bed, and before leaving him makes him promise to knock on the partition that separates her room from his, should he require anything during the night. He knocks, and she comes again to him. But that night and for many nights he suffered. That suffering he interprets as the obscure, organic, humble refusal on the part of those elements that represented all that was best in his life to accept the possibility of a formula in which they would have no part. This reluctance to die, this long and desperate and daily resistance before the perpetual exfoliation of personality, explains also his horror at the idea of ever living without Gilberte Swann, of ever losing his parents, at the idea of his own death. But this terror at the thought of separation—from Gilberte, from his parents, from himself—is dissipated in a greater terror, when he thinks that to the pain of separation will succeed indifference, that the privation will cease to be a privation when the alchemy of Habit has transformed the individual capable of suffering into a stranger for whom the motives of that suffering are an idle tale, when not only the objects of his affection have vanished, but also that affection itself ; and he thinks how absurd is our dream of a Paradise with retention of personality, since our life is a succession of Paradises successively denied, that the only true Paradise is the Paradise that has been lost, and that death will cure many of the desire for immortality.

The second episode that I have chosen as an illustration of the pact waived engages the same two characters, the narrator and his grandmother. He has been staying at Doncières with his friend Saint-Loup. He telephones to his grandmother in Paris. (After reading the description of this telephone call and its hardly less powerful corollary, when, years later, he speaks over the telephone with Albertine on returning home late after his first visit to the Princesse de Guermantes, Cocteau's *Voix Humaine* seems not merely a banality but an unnecessary banality.) After the conventional misunderstanding with the Vigilant Virgins (*sic*) of the central exchange, he hears his grandmother's voice, or what he assumes to be her voice, because he hears it now for the first time, in all its purity and reality, so different from the voice that he had been accustomed to follow on the open score of her face that he does not recognise it as hers. It is a grievous voice, its fragility unmitigated

14

and undisguised by the carefully arranged mask of her features, and this strange real voice is the measure of its owner's suffering. He hears it also as the symbol of her isolation, of their separation, as impalpable as a voice from the dead. The voice stops. His grandmother seems as irretrievably lost as Eurydice among the shades. Alone before the mouthpiece he calls her name in vain. Nothing can persuade him to remain at Doncières. He must see his grandmother. He leaves for Paris. He surprises her reading her beloved Mme. de Sévigné. But he is not there because she does not know that he is there. He is present at his own absence. And, in consequence of his journey and his anxiety, his habit is in abeyance, the habit of his tenderness for his grandmother. His gaze is no longer the necromancy that sees in each precious object a mirror of the past. The notion of what he should see has not had time to interfere its prism between the eye and its object. His eye functions with the cruel precision of a camera ; it photographs the reality of his grandmother. And he realises with horror that his grandmother is dead, long since and many times, that the cherished familiar of his mind, mercifully composed all along the years by the solicitude of habitual memory, exists no longer, that this mad old woman, drowsing over her book, overburdened with years, flushed and coarse and vulgar, is a stranger whom he has never seen.

The respite is brief. ' Of all human plants,' writes Proust, ' Habit requires the least fostering, and is the first to appear on the seeming desolation of the most barren rock.' Brief, and dangerously painful. The fundamental duty of Habit, about which it describes the futile and stupefying arabesques of its supererogations, consists in a perpetual adjustment and readjustment of our organic sensibility to the conditions of its worlds. Suffering represents the omission of that duty, whether through negligence or inefficiency, and boredom its adequate performance. The pendulum oscillates between these two terms : Suffering—that opens a window on the real and is the main condition of the artistic experience, and Boredom—with its host of top-hatted and hygienic ministers, Boredom that must be considered as the most tolerable because the most durable of human evils. Considered as a progression, this endless series of renovations leaves us as indifferent as the heterogeneity of any one of its terms, and the inconsequence of any given me disturbs us as little as the comedy of substitution. Indeed, we take as little cognisance of one as of the other, unless, vaguely, after the event, or clearly, when, as in the case of Proust, two birds in the bush are of infinitely greater value than one in the hand, and because—if I may add this nox vomica to an apéritif of metaphors—the heart of the cauliflower or the ideal core of the onion would represent a more appropriate tribute to the labours of poetical excavation than the crown of bay. I draw the conclusion of this matter from Proust's treasury of nutshell phrases : ' If there were no such thing as Habit, Life would of necessity appear delicious to all those whom Death would threaten at every moment, that is to say, to all Mankind.'

*　*
*

Proust had a bad memory—as he had an inefficient habit, because he had an inefficient habit. The man with a good memory does not remember anything because he does not forget anything. His memory is uniform, a creature of routine, at once a condition and function of his impeccable habit, an instrument of reference instead of an instrument of discovery. The pæan of his memory : ' I remember as well as I remember yesterday . . .' is also its epitaph, and gives the precise expression of its value. He cannot *remember* yesterday any more than he can remember to-morrow. He can contemplate yesterday hung out to dry with the wettest August bank holiday on record a little further down the clothes-line. Because his memory is a clothes-line and the images of his past dirty linen redeemed and the infallibly complacent servants of his reminiscential needs. Memory is obviously conditioned by perception. Curiosity is a non-

conditioned reflex, in its most primitive manifestations a reaction before a danger-stimulus, and seldom
exempt, even in its superior and apparently most
disinterested form, from utilitarian considerations.
Curiosity is the hair of our habit tending to stand on
end. It rarely happens that our attention is not
stained in greater or lesser degree by this animal
element. Curiosity is the safeguard, not the death, of
the cat, whether in skirts or on all fours. The more
interested our interest, the more indelible must be its
record of impressions. Its booty will always be available, because its aggression was a form of self-defence,
i.e. the function of an invariable. In extreme cases
memory is so closely related to habit that its word
takes flesh, and is not merely available in cases of
urgency, but habitually enforced. Thus absence of
mind is fortunately compatible with the active presence of our organs of articulation. I repeat that
rememoration, in its highest sense, cannot be applied
to these extracts of our anxiety. Strictly speaking,
we can only remember what has been registered by
our extreme inattention and stored in that ultimate
and inaccessible dungeon of our being to which Habit
does not possess the key, and does not need to, because it contains none of the hideous and useful
paraphernalia of war. But here, in that ' gouffre
interdit à nos sondes,' is stored the essence of ourselves, the best of our many selves and their concre-

tions that simplists call the world, the best because accumulated slyly and painfully and patiently under the nose of our vulgarity, the fine essence of a smothered divinity whose whispered ' disfazione ' is drowned in the healthy bawling of an all-embracing appetite, the pearl that may give the lie to our carapace of paste and pewter. May—when we escape into the spacious annexe of mental alienation, in sleep or the rare dispensation of waking madness. From this deep source Proust hoisted his world. His work is not an accident, but its salvage is an accident. The conditions of that accident will be revealed at the peak of this prevision. A second-hand climax is better than none. But no purpose can be served by withholding the name of the diver. Proust calls him ' involuntary memory.' The memory that is not memory, but the application of a concordance to the Old Testament of the individual, he calls ' voluntary memory.' This is the uniform memory of intelligence ; and it can be relied on to reproduce for our gratified inspection those impressions of the past that were consciously and intelligently formed. It has no interest in the mysterious element of inattention that colours our most commonplace experiences. It presents the past in monochrome. The images it chooses are as arbitrary as those chosen by imagination, and are equally remote from reality. Its action has been compared by Proust to that of turning the leaves of an album of photographs. The material that it furnishes contains nothing of the past, merely a blurred and uniform projection once removed of our anxiety and opportunism—that is to say, nothing. There is no great difference, says Proust, between the memory of a dream and the memory of reality. When the sleeper awakes, this emissary of his habit assures him that his 'personality' has not disappeared with his fatigue. It is possible (for those that take an interest in such speculations) to consider the resurrection of the soul as a final piece of impertinence from the same source. It insists on that most necessary, wholesome and monotonous plagiarism—the plagiarism of oneself. This thoroughgoing democrat makes no distinction between the 'Pensées' of Pascal and a soap advertisement. In fact, if Habit is the Goddess of Dulness, voluntary memory is Shadwell, and of Irish extraction. Involuntary memory is explosive, 'an immediate, total and delicious deflagration.' It restores, not merely the past object, but the Lazarus that it charmed or tortured, not merely Lazarus and the object, but more because less, more because it abstracts the useful, the opportune, the accidental, because in its flame it has consumed Habit and all its works, and in its brightness revealed what the mock reality of experience never can and never will reveal—the real. But involuntary memory is an unruly magician and will not be importuned. It chooses its own time and place for the performance of its miracle. I do not know how often this miracle recurs in Proust. I think twelve or thirteen times. But the first—the famous episode of the madeleine steeped in tea—would justify the assertion that his entire book is a monument to involuntary memory and the epic of its action. The whole of Proust's world comes out of a teacup, and not merely Combray and his childhood. For Combray brings us to the two ' ways ' and to Swann, and to Swann may be related every element of the Proustian experience and consequently its climax in revelation. Swann is behind Balbec, and Balbec is Albertine and Saint-Loup. Directly he involves Odette and Gilberte, the Verdurins and their clan, the music of Vinteuil and the magical prose of Bergotte ; indirectly (via Balbec and Saint-Loup) the Guermantes, Oriane and the Duke, the Princesse and M. de Charlus. Swann is the corner-stone of the entire structure, and the central figure of the narrator's childhood, a childhood that involuntary memory, stimulated or charmed by the long-forgotten taste of a madeleine steeped in an infusion of tea, conjures in all the relief and colour of its essential significance from the shallow well of a cup's inscrutable banality.

* *
*

From this Janal, trinal, agile monster or Divinity :
Time—a condition of resurrection because an instrument of death ; Habit—an infliction in so far as it
opposes the dangerous exaltation of the one and a
blessing in so far as it palliates the cruelty of the
other ; Memory—a clinical laboratory stocked with
poison and remedy, stimulant and sedative : from
Him the mind turns to the one compensation and
miracle of evasion tolerated by His tyranny and vigilance. This accidental and fugitive salvation in the
midst of life may supervene when the action of involuntary memory is stimulated by the negligence or
agony of Habit, and under no other circumstances,
nor necessarily then. Proust has adopted this mystic
experience as the Leitmotiv of his composition. It
recurs, like the red phrase of the Vinteuil Septuor, a
neuralgia rather than a theme, persistent and monotonous, disappears beneath the surface and emerges
a still finer and more nervous structure, enriched with
a strange and necessary incrustation of grace-notes, a
more confident and essential statement of reality, and
climbs through a series of precisions and purifications
to the pinnacle from which it commands and clarifies
the most humble incident of its ascent and delivers its
triumphant ultimatum. It appears for the first time
as the episode of the madeleine, and again on at least
five capital occasions before its final and multiple in-
vestment of the Guermantes Hotel at the opening of

the second volume of *Le Temps Retrouvé*, its culminating and integral expression. Thus the germ of the Proustian solution is contained in the statement of the problem itself. The source and point of departure of this ' sacred action,' the elements of communion, are provided by the physical world, by some immediate and fortuitous act of perception. The process is almost one of intellectualised animism. The following is the list of fetishes :

1. The madeleine steeped in an infusion of tea.
   (*Du Côté de Chez Swann*, i. 69-73.)
2. The steeples of Martinville, seen from Dr. Percepied's trap. (*Ibid.*, 258-262.)
3. A musty smell in a public lavatory in the Champs Elysées.
   (*A l'Ombre des Jeunes Filles en Fleurs*, i. 90.)
4. The three trees, seen near Balbec from the carriage of Mme. de Villeparisis. (*Ibid.*, ii. 161.)
5. The hedge of hawthorn near Balbec.
   (*Ibid.*, iii. 215.)
6. He stoops to unbutton his boots on the occasion of his second visit to the Grand Hotel at Balbec.
   (*Sodome et Gomorrhe*, ii. 176.)
7. Uneven cobbles in the courtyard of the Guermantes Hotel. (*Le Temps Retrouvé*, ii. 7.)
8. The noise of a spoon against a plate.
   (*Ibid.*, 9.)
9. He wipes his mouth with a napkin.
   (*Ibid.*, 10.)
10. The noise of water in the pipes. (*Ibid.*, 18.)
11. George Sand's *François le Champi*. (*Ibid.*, 30.)

The list is not complete. I have not included a number of tentative and abortive experiences, no one of which constitutes properly a recurrence of the motif, but rather a premonition of its approach. Of these shadowy, incomplete evocations a certain cluster of three is specially significant (*Côté de Guermantes*, ii. 80-82). He is waiting at home for Mlle. de Stermaria (who might have been the narrator's Albertine if she had not failed him then). He is transported successively to Balbec, Doncières and Combray by the twilight perceived above the curtains of his window, the descent of the stairs side by side with Robert de Saint-Loup who has just arrived, and the dense fog that has settled on the street. These three evocations, although incomplete, are intensely violent, and for a moment he is conscious of the heterogeneous matter and substance of these periods of his past : of the sombre, rugged sandstone of Combray, as opposed to the compact, glittering, translucid, rose-veined alabaster of Rivebelle. But he is not alone, he is interrupted by Saint-Loup, and what might have been the turning-point in his life, the climax that is not to be reached until many years later in the courtyard and library of the Princesse de Guermantes, is nothing more than one of its most fugitive precursors.

The last five visitations—cobbles, spoon and plate, napkin, water in the pipes, and *François le Champi*—may be considered as forming a single annunciation and as providing the key to his life and work. The sixth capital experience is particularly important (although less familiar than the famous madeleine, which is invariably quoted as the type of the Proustian revelation) as representing not only a central appearance of the motif but also an application of the erratic machinery of habit and memory as conceived by Proust. Albertine and the Proustian *Discours de la Méthode* having waited so long can wait a little longer, and the reader is cordially invited to omit this summary analysis of what is perhaps the greatest passage that Proust ever wrote—*Les Intermittences du Cœur*.

This incident takes place on the first evening of the narrator's second visit to Balbec. On this occasion he is with his mother, his grandmother having died a year before. But the dead annex the quick as surely as the Kingdom of France annexes the Duchy of Orléans. His mother has become his grandmother, whether through the suggestion of regret or an idolatrous cult of the dead or the disintegrating effect of loss that breaks the chrysalis and hastens the metamorphosis of an atavistic embryo whose maturation is slow and imperceptible without the stimulus of grief. She carries her mother's bag and her muff, and is never without a volume of Mme. de Sévigné. She who formerly chaffed her mother for never writing a letter without quoting Mme. de Sévigné or Mme. de Beausergent, builds now her own to her son around some phrase from the Letters or the Memoirs. The narrator's motives for this second visit are not those—furnished by Swann and his fantasy—that granted him no peace while Balbec had still the mystery and beauty of its name, before reality had replaced the mirage of imagination by the mirage of memory and explained away the value of the unknown as Venice will in due course be explained away and the odyssey of the local ' tacot ' through a mythical land by the etymology of Brichot and the appeasing contempt of familiarity. The Persian church with its stained glass ' surfed in spray ' and its steeple hewn out of the granite rampart of a Norman cliff has been replaced by the Giorgionesque chambermaid of Mme. de Putbus.

He arrives tired and ill, as on the former occasion that has been analysed as an example of the death of Habit. Now, however, the dragon has been reduced to docility, and the cavern is a room. Habit has been reorganised—an operation described by Proust as ' longer and more difficult than the turning inside out of an eyelid, and which consists in the imposition of our own familiar soul on the terrifying soul of our surroundings.' He stoops down—cautiously, in the interests of his heart—to unbutton his boots. Suddenly he is filled with a divine familiar presence.

26

Once more he is restored to himself by that being whose tenderness, several years earlier, in a similar moment of distress and fatigue, had brought him a moment's calm, by his grandmother as she had been then, as she had continued to be until that fatal day of her stroke in the Champs Elysées, after which nothing remained of her but a name, so that her death was of as little consequence to the narrator as the death of a stranger. Now, a year after her burial, thanks to the mysterious action of involuntary memory, he learns that she is dead. At any given moment our total soul, in spite of its rich balance-sheet, has only a fictitious value. Its assets are never completely realisable. But he has not merely extracted from this gesture the lost reality of his grandmother : he has recovered the lost reality of himself, the reality of his lost self. As though the figure of Time could be represented by an endless series of parallels, his life is switched over to another line and proceeds, without any solution of continuity, from that remote moment of his past when his grandmother stooped over his distress. And he is as incapable of visualising the incidents that punctuated that long period of intermittence, the incidents of the past few hours, as in that interval he was inexorably bereft of that precious panel in the tapestry of his days representing his grandmother and his love for her. But this resumption of a past life is poisoned by a cruel anachronism : his grandmother is dead. For the first time since her death, since the Champs Elysées, he has recovered her living and complete, as she was so many times, at Combray and Paris and Balbec. For the first time since her death he knows that she is dead, he knows *who* is dead. He had to recover her alive and tender before he could admit her dead and for ever incapable of any tenderness. This contradiction between presence and irremediable obliteration is intolerable. Not merely the memory —the experience—of their mutual predestination is retrospectively abolished by the certainty that it is folly to speak in such cases of predestination, that his grandmother was a chance acquaintance and the few years spent with her an accident, that as he meant nothing to her before their meeting, so he can mean nothing to her after her departure. He cannot understand ' this dolorous synthesis of survival and annihilation.' And he writes : ' I did not know whether this painful and for the moment incomprehensible impression would ever yield up any truth. But I knew that if I ever did succeed in extracting some truth from the world, it would be from such an impression and from none other, an impression at once particular and spontaneous, which had neither been formed by my intelligence nor attenuated by my pusillanimity, but whose double and mysterious furrow had been carved, as by a thunderbolt, within me, by the inhuman and supernatural blade of Death, or the revelation of Death.' But already will, the will to live, the will not to suffer, Habit, having recovered from its momentary paralysis, has laid the foundations of its evil and necessary structure, and the vision of his grandmother begins to fade and to lose that miraculous relief and clarity that no effort of deliberate rememoration can impart or restore. It is redeemed for a moment by the sight of that party-wall which, like an instrument, had transmitted the faltering statement of his distress, and, some days later, by the drawing of a blind in a railway carriage, when the evocation of his grandmother is so vivid and painful that he is obliged to abandon his visit to Mme. Verdurin and leave the train. But before this new brightness, this old brightness revived and intensified, can be finally extinguished, the Calvary of pity and remorse must be trod. The insistent memory of cruelties to one who is dead is a flagellation, because the dead are only dead in so far as they continue to exist in the heart of the survivor. And pity for what has been suffered is a more cruel and precise expression for that suffering than the conscious estimate of the sufferer, who is spared at least one despair—the despair of the spectator. The narrator recalls an incident that took place during his first stay at Balbec, in the light of which he had considered his grandmother as a frivolous and vain old woman. She had insisted on having her photograph taken by Saint-Loup, so that her beloved grandchild might have at least that poor record of her latter days, a fusillade of syncopes (called ' symcopes ' by the manager of the Grand Hotel, who now reveals to the narrator this first onslaught of his grandmother's malady and unwittingly provides, in his absurd malapropism, yet another instrument of painful evocation) and strokes having allowed her to see death clearly at last as a coming event. And she had been very particular about her pose and the inclination of her hat, wishing the photograph to be one of a grandmother and not of a disease. All of which precautions the narrator had translated as the futilities of coquetry. So, unlike Miranda, he suffers with her whom he had not seen suffer, as though, for him as for Françoise, whom Giotto's charitable scullion in childbirth and the violent translation of what is fit to live into what is fit to eat leave indifferent, but who cannot restrain her tears when informed that there has been an earthquake in China, pain could only be focussed at a distance.

*　　*

*

The Albertine tragedy is prepared during the narrator's first stay at Balbec, involved by their relations in Paris, consolidated during his second stay at Balbec, and consummated by her imprisonment in Paris. She appears to him for the first time, absorbed in the radiance of the 'little band' at Balbec, pushing a bicycle, an item in that ineffable and inaccessible procession, winding and unwinding its gracious figures against the sea, and seeming to the envious adoration of the narrator as eternally and hermetically exclusive as a frieze or a frescoed cortège. She has no individuality. She is merely one blossom in this fragile hedge of Pennsylvanian roses breaking the line of the waves, and this original collective mystery of the little band enables him many years later, when Albertine has been detached and made a captive, when the nebulae of this constellation have been synthesised into one single astral obsession, to deny, not merely the objective reality (as was the case with Gilberte) of his love for her, but also its subjective reality, by co-ordinating her with another image. She looks at him one day on the shore (the identification with Albertine is retrospective), and he writes : 'I knew that I would not possess this young cyclist if I did not possess what was in her eyes.' His imagination weaves its cocoon about this frail and almost abstract chrysalis, this unit in an orgiac band of cycling Bacchanti. He is introduced to her by the painter Elstir, and proceeds to her acquaintance by a series of subtractions, each fragment of his fantasy and desire being replaced by an infinitely less precious notion. Thus her relationship with Mme. Bontemps, her early amiabilities, the effect of a declamatory beauty-spot on her chin, her use of the adverb ' perfectly ' for ' quite,' the provisional inflammation of her temple constituting an optical centre of gravity about which the composition of her features is organised, are sufficient taken together to establish an Albertine as remote from the first Albertine, the beach flower, as yet a third aspect, characterised by a pronounced nasal enunciation, a terrifying command of slang, the disappearance of the inflamed temple, and the miraculous transference of the beauty-spot from her chin to her upper lip, is remote from the second. Thus is established the *pictorial* multiplicity of Albertine that will duly evolve into a *plastic* and moral multiplicity, no longer a mere shifting superficies and an effect of the observer's angle of approach rather than the expression of an inward and active variety, but a multiplicity in depth, a turmoil of objective and immanent contradictions over which the subject has no control. Yet already he concludes, before the kaleidoscope of her expressions, before this face that from being all surface, smooth and waxed, passes to an almost fluid state of translucid gaiety, and from the chiselled polish of an opal to the feverish black-red congestion of a cyclamen, that the Name is an example of a barbarous society's primitivism, and as conventionally inadequate as ' Homer ' or ' sea.'

His first vague gesture of approach is coldly repulsed. He concludes that Albertine is virtuous and that his original hypothesis—that she was possibly the mistress of a racing cyclist or a champion boxer—was not merely incorrect in its specific application but based on an entirely false sense of her character. He concludes that Albertine is virtuous, and his first stay at Balbec closes on that impression.

It is corrected by a visit from Albertine in Paris. To a new vocabulary, garnished with such sophistications as ' distinguished,' ' to my mind,' ' mousmê,' ' lapse of time,' corresponds a new and sophisticated Albertine, as lavish now of her favours as she was formerly parsimonious. The narrator, while supposing that Albertine has been the object of an initiation, can establish no common measure between these three main aspects of Albertine : the passionate unreal Albertine of the shore, the real and virginal Albertine such as she appeared to him at the end of his stay at Balbec, and now this third Albertine that fulfils the promise of the first in the reality of the second. ' My surplus of knowledge ended in a provisional agnosticism. What affirmation was possible when the original hypothesis had first been refuted and then confirmed ? ' And the pleasure he takes with Albertine is intensified by the reaching out of his spirit towards that immaterial reality that she seems to symbolise, Balbec and its sea—' as though the material possession of an object, residence in a town, were the equivalent of spiritual possession.' This compound object of desire—a woman and the sea—is simplified of its second element by the habit of the first. A secondary compound can be formed by jealousy, and the amalgam of human and marine restored, but as a cardiac and no longer as a visual stimulus. But even this new Albertine is multiple, and just as the most modern applications of photography can frame a single church successively in the arcades of all the others and the entire horizon in the arch of a bridge or between two adjacent leaves, thus decomposing the illusion of a solid object into its manifold component aspects, so the short journey of his lips to the cheek of Albertine creates ten Albertines, and transforms a human banality into a manyheaded goddess. But the menace of what life with her must be is announced to him more clearly when, after his first visit to the Princesse de Guermantes, he sits alone in his room waiting for Albertine (who, momentarily eclipsed by the mysterious Mlle. de Stermaria, has been absent from his mind all evening), for Albertine who has promised to come and who does not come and whose non-arrival exalts a simple physical irritation into a flame of moral anguish, so that he listens for her step or for the sublime summons of the telephone, not with his ear and mind, but with his heart. For in his anxiety he

has added yet another crystal to this branch of Salz-
bourg, the crystal of a need, of that need that tortured
him at Combray and that only his mother could allay
with the host of her lips.   But when she telephones to
explain, when he knows that she is on her way, then
he wonders how he could have seen in this vulgar
Albertine, similar, even inferior, to so many others,
a source of comfort and salvation that no miracle
could replace.   ' One only loves that which is not
possessed, one only loves that in which one pursues
the inaccessible.'

The second visit to Balbec, inaugurated by the
retrospective loss and mourning of his grandmother,
completes the transformation of a creature of surface
into a creature of depth—unfathomable, accomplishes the solidification of a profile.   From the moment that Dr. Cottard sees Albertine and her friend
Andrée (one of the band) dancing together in the
Casino at Incarville, and pompously diagnoses a case
of sexual perversion, dates the ' reciprocal torture ' of
their relations.   From this point lies and counterlies,
pursuit and evasion, and on the part of the narrator a
love for Albertine whose intensity is related in direct
proportion to the success of her prevarications.   Because Albertine is not only a liar as all those that
believe themselves loved are liars : she is a natural
liar.   A succession of incidents consolidate the narrator's doubt on the chapter of Albertine, that is to

say, exasperate his love for her. She fails to keep an appointment, she lies about an appointment with a mythical friend of her aunt at Infreville, she stares at the reflection in a mirror of Mlle. Bloch and her cousin, two practising Sapphists, and then denies having seen them. Then, the narrator's jealousy and sense of impotence being at their height, there follows a lull, and he is calmed by the docility of an always available Albertine. He becomes indifferent to this new creature who opposes no further resistance. He resolves to break with her, and announces his decision to his mother. Returning one evening with Albertine in the ' tacot ' from a party at La Raspelière he goes over in his mind the formulae of separation. He happens to mention that he is interested in the music of Vinteuil. Albertine, whose taste in music is as primitive as her appreciation of painting and architecture is developed, hoping to create a favourable impression, declares that she is perfectly familiar with the music of Vinteuil, thanks to her intimacy with Mlle. Vinteuil and her friend, the actress Léa. In a paroxysm of jealousy the narrator is back again at Montjouvain, the horrified spectator of these two Lesbians flavouring their pleasure in a sadistic act of desecration at the expense of M. Vinteuil himself, who has been dead some time.[1] And this vision of Montjouvain seems to come like Orestes to avenge

[1] *Du Côté de Chez Swann*, i.

the murder of Agamemnon. And he thinks of his grandmother and of his cruelties towards her. Albertine, so remote and detached from his heart a moment before, is now not merely an obsession, but part of himself, within him, and the movement she makes to descend from the train threatens to tear open his body. He forces her to accompany him to Balbec. The strand and the waves exist no more, the summer is dead. The sea is a veil that cannot hide the horror of Montjouvain, the intolerable vision of sadistic lubricity and a photograph defiled. He sees in Albertine another Rachel and another Odette, and the sterility and mockery of an affection dictated by interest. He sees his life as a succession of joyless dawns, poisoned by the tortures of memory and isolation. The next morning he brings Albertine to Paris and locks her up in his house.

His life in common with Albertine is volcanic, his mind torn by a series of eruptions : Fury, Jealousy, Envy, Curiosity, Suffering, Pride, Honour and Love. The form of this last is pre-established by the arbitrary images of memory and imagination, an artificial fiction to which, and for his suffering, he forces the woman to conform. The person of Albertine counts for nothing. She is not a motive, but a notion, as far removed from reality as the portrait of Odette by Elstir, which is the portrait not of the beloved but of the love that has deformed her, is removed from the

37

real Odette. So that his anxiety cannot be argued from Albertine, but from a whole processus of sufferings and emotions that have been associated with her person and attached to it by habit. His life with Albertine, containing not one single positive advantage, is no more than an appeasement, the token of a monopoly. And not always an appeasement, because the mystery of Albertine persists, the mystery that he sensed in her eyes when they first met before the sea at Balbec, the mystery that charmed him then and that now, because it represents the fragility of his domination, he longs to efface. This last phase of his association with Albertine bears the trace of its inception, its inception in his jealousy and her deceitfulness. 'How have we the courage to wish to live, how can we make a movement to preserve ourselves from death, in a world where love is provoked by a lie and consists solely in the need of having our sufferings appeased by whatever being has made us suffer?' Surely in the whole of literature there is no study of that desert of loneliness and recrimination that men call love posed and developed with such diabolical unscrupulousness. After this, *Adolphe* is a petulant dribbling, the mock epic of salivary hypersecretion, Mme. de Cambremer (whose name, as Oriane de Guermantes observes to Swann, stops just in time) in tears. Every word and gesture of Albertine are caught up in the vortex of jealousy and suspicion, translated and

mistranslated, reapplied and misapplied. Every re-
membered incident is decomposed in the acid of his
mistrust. 'My imagination provided equations for
the unknown in this algebra of desire.' But Albertine is a fugitive, and no expression of her value can
be complete unless preceded by some such symbol as
that which in physics denotes speed. A static Albertine would soon be conquered, would soon be compared to all the other possible conquests that her
possession excludes, and the infinite of what is not
and may be preferred to the nullity of what is. Love,
he insists, can only coexist with a state of dissatisfac-
tion, whether born of jealousy or its predecessor—
desire. It represents our demand for a whole. Its
inception and its continuance imply the consciousness
that something is lacking. 'One only loves that
which one does not possess entirely.' And until the
rupture takes place—(and indeed long after it has
taken place, even when the object is dead, thanks to
a retrospective jealousy, a 'jalousie de l'escalier')—
warfare. Albertine mentions casually that she may
visit the Verdurins. Anagram : ' I may go and see
the Verdurins to-morrow. I don't know. I don't
particularly want to.' Translation : ' It is absolutely certain that I will go and see the Verdurins to-
morrow. It is of the greatest possible importance.'
He remembers that Morel has promised to conduct
the Vinteuil Septuor for Mme. Verdurin, and con-

cludes that Mlle. Vinteuil and her friend will be among the guests, and that by some infernal stroke of cunning Albertine has made an appointment with them for the following evening. Thus these rare moments of relief that enable him to form the determination to break with Albertine and to put an end to this double slavery that prevents him from going to Venice, prevents him from working, separates him from his friends, and at most and grudgingly affords him the bitter satisfaction of knowing that no rival shall enjoy what he himself cannot enjoy—these rare periods of relative ease are cut short by the intervention of a new motive of jealousy or by the transformation, in the tireless crucible of his mind, of some insignificant detail of their past into a poison for the exasperation of his love or hate or jealousy (interchangeable terms) and the corrosion of his heart. For example, when he is at last resolved on separation, she swears that her aunt has no friend living at Infreville. There is no limit to her deceit and none to his faculty of suffering. And in the midst of this Tolomea he *knows* that this woman has no reality, that ' our most exclusive love for a person is always our love for something else,' that intrinsically she is less than nothing, but that in her nothingness there is active, mysterious and invisible, a current that forces him to bow down and worship an obscure and implacable Goddess, and to make sacrifices of himself before her. And the Goddess who requires this sacrifice and this humiliation, whose sole condition of patronage is corruptibility, and into whose faith and worship all mankind is born, is the Goddess of Time. No object prolonged in this temporal dimension tolerates possession, meaning by possession total possession, only to be achieved by the complete identification of object and subject. The impenetrability of the most vulgar and insignificant human creature is not merely an illusion of the subject's jealousy (although this impenetrability stands out more clearly under the Röntgen rays of a jealousy so fiercely hypertrophied as was that of the narrator, a jealousy that is doubtless a form of his domination complex and his infantilism, two tendencies highly developed in Proust). All that is active, all that is enveloped in time and space, is endowed with what might be described as an abstract, ideal and absolute impermeability. So that we can understand the position of Proust : ' We imagine that the object of our desire is a being that can be laid down before us, enclosed within a body. Alas ! it is the extension of that being to all the points of space and time that it has occupied and will occupy. If we do not possess contact with such a place and with such an hour we do not possess that being. But we cannot touch all these points.' And again : ' A being scattered in space and time is no longer a woman but a series of events on which we can throw no light, a series of problems that cannot be solved, a sea that, like Xerxes, we thrash with rods in an absurd desire to punish it for having engulfed our treasure.' And he defines love as : ' Time and Space made perceptible to the heart.' He persuades Albertine to go to a special performance at the Trocadéro instead of to the Verdurin reception. She consents. The Vinteuil menace having been averted, he thinks of Albertine as an importunity. He is idly turning the leaves of the *Figaro* when he is suddenly galvanised by the announcement that Léa is acting at that very gala performance to which he has sent Albertine. Gala ! In a frenzy he sends Françoise to bring her back. She returns without having been able to speak to Léa. His calm is restored and again shattered by an allusion made by Albertine to the Buttes-Chaumont. He suspects Andrée. He sees that there can be no peace and no rest until Albertine has gone. He will forget her as he forgot Gilberte Swann and the Duchesse de Guermantes. (But Gilberte is to Albertine what the Sonata is to the Septuor—an experiment.) And the idea that his suffering will cease is more unbearable than that suffering itself. ' The lion of my love trembled before the python of forgetfulness.' Early one morning, during a period of calm, he makes up his mind. Albertine must leave him. He loves her no longer. He will go to Venice and forget her. He

rings for Françoise to send out for a guide and a time-
table. He will go to Venice to his dream of Gothic
time on a vernal sea. Enter Françoise. 'Mlle.
Albertine left at nine o'clock and gave me this letter
for Monsieur.' And like Phèdre, he recognises the
ever-wakeful Gods.

> '. . . ces dieux qui dans mon flanc
> Ont allumé le feu fatal à tout mon sang,
> Ces dieux qui se sont fait une gloire cruelle
> De réduire le cœur d'une faible mortelle.'

Shortly afterwards Albertine is killed in Touraine.
Her death, her emancipation from Time, does not
calm his jealousy nor accelerate the extinction of an
obsession whose rack and wheel were the days and
the hours. They and their love were amphibious,
plunged in the past and the present. There is a
moral climate and a sentimental calendar, where the
instrument of commensuration is not solar but cardiac.
To forget Albertine he must—like a man struck down
by hemiplegia—forget the seasons, their seasons,
and, like a child, learn them anew. ' In order to be
consoled I would have to forget, not one, but in-
numerable Albertines.' And not only 'I,' but the
many 'I's. For any given Albertine there exists a
correlative narrator, and no anachronism can put
apart what Time has coupled. He must return and
re-enact the stations of a diminishing suffering. Thus
his astonishment that Albertine, so alive within him,

can be dead—the fact of her life assailed by the notion of her death—gives way to the less painful astonishment that one who is dead can continue to concern him—the fact of her death assailed by the notion of her life. But the stations of this inverted Calvary retain their original dynamism, their crescendo, their tension towards a cross. At each halt he suffers from the hallucination that what has been left behind is still before him. ' Such is the cruelty of memory.' He describes three of these stages, arranged in descending powers of brutality. The first, a solitary walk in the Bois de Boulogne, when every female figure is an Albertine, the astral synthesis of the bright and riotous band at Balbec paling now and breaking up, with an inverse symmetry, into its nebulae ; the second, a conversation with Andrée, who reveals the full treachery and misery of her friend's life ; and finally in Venice, when a telegram from Gilberte announcing her engagement to Robert de Saint-Loup is signed ' Albertine ' through a misreading of Gilberte's vulgar and pretentious orthography. But this Albertine risen from the dead cannot trouble her real sepulchre, the only inviolate sepulchre, in the unkempt cemetery of the heart. Albertine is the first and the last, the Bacchante of the shore, as seen by the narrator in that pure act of understanding—intuition, and the captive that has recovered liberty and life, possessed of herself among

44

the young laundresses, bathing in the Loire. This final confirmation of the original perspective is typical of Proust's characterisation. Thus there is a suggestion of congruence between the final Duchesse de Guermantes, as she appears at the matinée of her cousin, and the gently wanton descendant of Geneviève de Brabant, exposed for the first time to the narrator's adoration in the church of St. Hilaire at Combray, following mass in the chapel of Gilbert the Bad, her eyes of periwinkle smiling and restless and the colour of the sunlight filtering through his window or of the girdle of Geneviève herself, and bathed in the mystery of Merovingian time and the amaranth and legendary radiance of her name. And Gilberte herself emerges from her successive transformations, from the Gilberte Swann of the Champs Elysées, Mlle. de Forcheville after the death of Swann, Mme. de Saint-Loup, and finally, by the death of Robert, Duchesse de Guermantes, as first seen at Tansonville through a trellis of red hawthorn, an impudent nymph leaning on her spade, amidst the jasmine and the copper wallflowers. And he sees his love for Albertine as a testimony to his original clairvoyance and an affirmation, in spite of the denegations of his reason, of that vision of her as a rapacious and elusive gull, hostile and remote against the sea. ' In the midst of the most complete blindness, perspicacity subsists in the form of tenderness and predilection.

So that it is a mistake to speak of an evil choice in love, since the very fact of there having been a choice implies that it has been an evil one.' And as before, wisdom consists in obliterating the faculty of suffering rather than in a vain attempt to reduce the stimuli that exasperate that faculty. ' Non che la speme, il desiderio . . .' 'One desires to be understood because one desires to be loved, and one desires to be loved because one loves. We are indifferent to the understanding of others, and their love is an importunity.'

But if love, for Proust, is a function of man's sadness, friendship is a function of his cowardice ; and, if neither can be realised because of the impenetrability (isolation) of all that is not ' cosa mentale,' at least the failure to possess may have the nobility of that which is tragic, whereas the attempt to communicate where no communication is possible is merely a simian vulgarity, or horribly comic, like the madness that holds a conversation with the furniture. Friendship, according to Proust, is the negation of that irremediable solitude to which every human being is condemned. Friendship implies an almost piteous acceptance of face values. Friendship is a social expedient, like upholstery or the distribution of garbage buckets. It has no spiritual significance. For the artist, who does not deal in surfaces, the rejection of friendship is not only reasonable, but a necessity. Because the only possible spiritual development is in the sense of depth. The artistic tendency is not expansive, but a contraction. And art is the apotheosis of solitude. There is no communication because there are no vehicles of communication. Even on the rare occasions when word and gesture happen to be valid expressions of personality, they lose their significance on their passage through the cataract of the personality that is opposed to them. Either we speak and act for ourselves—in which case speech and action are distorted and emptied of their meaning by an intelligence that is not ours, or else we speak and act for others—in which case we speak and act a lie. 'One lies all one's life long,' writes Proust, 'notably to those that love one, and above all to that stranger whose contempt would cause one most pain—oneself.' Yet surely the scorn of half a dozen—or half a million—sincere imbeciles for a man of genius ought to cure us of our absurd puntiglio and our capacity for being affected by that abridged libel that we call an insult.

Proust situates friendship somewhere between fatigue and ennui. He does not agree with the Nietzschean conception that friendship must be based on intellectual sympathy, because he does not see friendship as having the least intellectual significance. 'We agree with those whose ideas (non-Platonic) are at the same degree of confusion as our own.' For him the exercise of friendship is tantamount to a

47

sacrifice of that only real and incommunicable essence of oneself to the exigencies of a frightened habit whose confidence requires to be restored by a dose of attention. It represents a false movement of the spirit—from within to without, from the spiritual assimilation of the immaterial as provided by the artist, as extracted by him from life, to the abject and indigestible husks of direct contact with the material and concrete, with what we call the material and the concrete. Thus he visits Balbec and Venice, meets Gilberte and the Duchesse de Guermantes and Albertine, attracted not by what they are but impelled by their arbitrary and ideal equivalents. The only fertile research is excavatory, immersive, a contraction of the spirit, a descent. The artist is active, but negatively, shrinking from the nullity of extracircumferential phenomena, drawn in to the core of the eddy. He cannot practise friendship, because friendship is the centrifugal force of self-fear, self-negation. Saint-Loup must be considered as more general than himself, as a product of the oldest French nobility, and the beauty and ease of his tenderness for the narrator—as when, for example, he accomplishes the most delicate and graceful gymnastics in a Paris restaurant so that his friend shall not be disturbed—are appreciated, not as the manifestations of a special and charming personality, but as the inevitable adjuncts of excessively good birth and breeding. ' Man, writes Proust, ' is not a building that can receive additions to its superficies, but a tree whose stem and leafage are an expression of inward sap.' We are alone. We cannot know and we cannot be known. ' Man is the creature that cannot come forth from himself, who knows others only in himself, and who, if he asserts the contrary, lies.'

Here, as always, Proust is completely detached from all moral considerations. There is no right and wrong in Proust nor in his world. (Except possibly in those passages dealing with the war, when for a space he ceases to be an artist and raises his voice with the plebs, mob, rabble, canaille). Tragedy is not concerned with human justice. Tragedy is the statement of an expiation, but not the miserable expiation of a codified breach of a local arrangement, organised by the knaves for the fools. The tragic figure represents the expiation of original sin, of the original and eternal sin of him and all his ' soci malorum,' the sin of having been born.

> ' Pues el delito mayor .
> Del hombre es haber nacido.'

*　*
*

Driving to the Guermantes Hotel he feels that everything is lost, that his life is a succession of losses, devoid of reality because nothing survives, nothing of his love for Gilberte, for the Duchesse de Guermantes, for his grandmother, and now nothing of his love for Albertine, nothing of Combray and Balbec and Venice except the distorted images of voluntary memory, a life all in length, a sequence of dislocations and adjustments, where neither mystery nor beauty is sacred, where all, except the adamantine columns of his enduring boredom, has been consumed in the torrential solvent of the years, a life so protracted in the past and so meaningless in the future, so utterly bereft of any individual and permanent necessity, that his death, now or to-morrow or in a year or in ten, would be a termination but not a conclusion. And he thinks how empty is Bergotte's phrase : ' the joys of the spirit.' For art, which he had so long believed the one ideal and inviolate element in a corruptible world, seems now, whether because of his incurable lack of talent or its own inherent artificiality, as unreal and sterile as the constructions of a demented imagination—' that insane barrel-organ that always plays the wrong tune ' ; and the materials of art—Beatrice and Faust and the ' azur du ciel immense et ronde ' and the seagirt cities—all the absolute beauty of a magic world, as vulgar and unworthy in their reality as Rachel and Cottard, and pale and weary and cruel and inconstant and joyless as Shelley's moon. So, after years of fruitless solitude, it is without enthusiasm that he drags himself back to a society that has long since ceased to interest him. And now, on the outskirts of this futility, favoured by the very depression and fatigue that had appeared to his disgust as the after-math of a minute and sterile lucidity (favoured, because the pretensions of a discouraged memory are for the moment reduced to the most immediate and utilitarian presentification), he is to receive the oracle that had invariably been denied to the most exalted tension of his spirit, which his intelligence had failed to extract from the sismic enigma of tree and flower and gesture and art, and suffer a religious experience in the only intelligible sense of that epithet, at once an assumption and an annunciation, so that at last he will understand the promise of Bergotte and the achievement of Elstir and the message of Vinteuil from his paradise and the dolorous and necessary course of his own life and the infinite futility—for the artist—of all that is not art.

This matinée is divided into two parts. The mystical experience and meditation of the narrator in the Cartesian hotcupboard of the Guermantes library, and the implications of that experience applied to the work of art that takes shape in his mind in the course of the reception itself. From the victory over Time he passes to the victory of Time, from the negation of Death to its affirmation. Thus, at the end as in the

51

body of his work, Proust respects the dual significance of every condition and circumstance of life. The most ideal tautology presupposes a relation and the affirmation of equality involves only an approximate identification, and by asserting unity denies unity.

Crossing the courtyard he stumbles on the cobbles. His surroundings vanish, wattmen, stables, carriages, guests, the entire reality of the place in its hour, his anxiety and doubts as to the reality of life and art disappear, he is stunned by waves of rapture, saturated in that same felicity that had irrigated so sparingly the desolation of his life. Drabness is obliterated in an intolerable brightness. And suddenly Venice emerges from the series of forgotten days, Venice whose radiant essence he had never been able to express because it had been rejected by the imperious vulgarity of a working-day memory, but which this chance reduplication of a precarious equilibrium in the Baptistry of San Marco has lifted from its Adriatic shore and set down, a bright and vehement interloper, in the courtyard of the Princesse de Guermantes. But already the vision has faded and he is free to resume his social functions. He is ushered into the library, because ex-Mme. Verdurin, at once the Norn and Victim of Harmonic Megrims, is enthroned in the midst of her guests, passionately absorbing Rino-Gomenol in the interests of her mucous membrane and suffering the most atrocious ecstasies of Stravinskian neuralgia. While he is waiting alone for the music to be over, the miracle of the courtyard is renewed under four different forms. They have already been referred to. A servant strikes a spoon against a plate, he wipes his mouth with a heavily starched napkin, the water cries like a siren in the pipes, he takes down *François le Champi* from the shelves. And just as the Piazza di San Marco burst its way into the courtyard and there asserted its luminous and fleeting domination, so now the library is successively invaded by a forest, the high tide breaking on the shore at Balbec, the vast dining-room of the Grand Hotel flooded, like an aquarium, with the sunset and the evening sea, and lastly Combray and its ' ways ' and the deferential transmission of a sour and distinguished prose, shaped and stated by his mother's voice, muted and sweetened almost to a lullaby, unwinding all night long its reassuring foil of sound before a child's insomnia.

The most successful evocative experiment can only project the echo of a past sensation, because, being an act of intellection, it is conditioned by the prejudices of the intelligence which abstracts from any given sensation, as being illogical and insignificant, a discordant and frivolous intruder, whatever word or gesture, sound or perfume, cannot be fitted into the puzzle of a concept. But the essence of any new experience is contained precisely in this mysterious element that the vigilant will rejects as an anachronism. It is the axis about which the sensation pivots, the centre of gravity of its coherence. So that no amount of voluntary manipulation can reconstitute in its integrity an impression that the will has—so to speak—buckled into incoherence. But if, *by accident*, and given favourable circumstances (a relaxation of the subject's habit of thought and a reduction of the radius of his memory, a generally diminished tension of consciousness following upon a phase of extreme discouragement), if by some miracle of analogy the central impression of a past sensation recurs as an immediate stimulus which can be instinctively identified by the subject with the model of duplication (*whose integral purity has been retained because it has been forgotten*), then the total past sensation, not its echo nor its copy, but the sensation itself, annihilating every spatial and temporal restriction, comes in a rush to engulf the subject in all the beauty of its infallible proportion. Thus the sound produced by a spoon struck against a plate is subconsciously identified by the narrator with the sound of a hammer struck by a mechanic against the wheel of a train drawn up before a wood, a sound that his will had rejected as extraneous to its immediate activity. But a subconscious and disinterested act of perception has reduced the object—the wood—to its immaterial and spiritually digestible equivalent, and the record of this pure act of cognition has not merely been associated with this sound of a hammer struck against a wheel, but centralised about it. The mood, as usual, has no importance. The point of departure of the Proustian exposition is not the crystalline agglomeration but its kernel—the crystallised. The most trivial experience—he says in effect—is encrusted with elements that logically are not related to it and have consequently been rejected by our intelligence : it is imprisoned in a vase filled with a certain perfume and a certain colour and raised to a certain temperature. These vases are suspended along the height of our years, and, not being accessible to our intelligent memory, are in a sense immune, the purity of their climatic content is guaranteed by forgetfulness, each one is kept at its distance, at its date. So that when the imprisoned microcosm is besieged in the manner described, we are flooded by a new air and a new perfume (new precisely because already experienced), and we breathe the true air of Paradise, of the only Paradise that is not the dream of a madman, the Paradise that has been lost.

The identification of immediate with past experience, the recurrence of past action or reaction in the present, amounts to a participation between the ideal and the real, imagination and direct apprehension, symbol and substance. Such participation frees the essential reality that is denied to the contemplative as to the active life. What is common to present and past is more essential than either taken separately. Reality, whether approached imaginatively or empirically, remains a surface, hermetic. Imagination, applied—a priori—to what is absent, is exercised in vacuo and cannot tolerate the limits of the real. Nor is any direct and purely experimental contact possible between subject and object, because they are automatically separated by the subject's consciousness of perception, and the object loses its purity and becomes a mere intellectual pretext or motive. But, thanks to this reduplication, the experience is at once imaginative and empirical, at once an evocation and a direct perception, real without being merely actual, ideal without being merely abstract, the ideal real, the essential, the extratemporal. But if this mystical experience communicates an extratemporal essence, it follows that the communicant is for the moment an extratemporal being. Consequently the Proustian solution consists, in so far as it has been examined, in the negation of Time and Death, the negation of Death because the negation of Time. Death is dead because Time is dead. (At this point a brief impertinence, which consists in considering *Le Temps Retrouvé* almost as inappropriate a description of the Proustian solution as *Crime and Punishment* of a masterpiece that contains no allusion to either crime or punishment. Time is not recovered, it is obliterated.

Time is recovered, and Death with it, when he
leaves the library and joins the guests, perched in
precarious decrepitude on the aspiring stilts of the
former and preserved from the latter by a miracle of
terrified equilibrium. If the title is a good title the
scene in the library is an anticlimax.) So now in the
exaltation of his brief eternity, having emerged from
the darkness of time and habit and passion and intelligence, he understands the necessity of art. For
in the brightness of art alone can be deciphered the
baffled ecstasy that he had known before the inscrutable superficies of a cloud, a triangle, a spire, a
flower, a pebble, when the mystery, the essence, the
Idea, imprisoned in matter, had solicited the bounty
of a subject passing by within the shell of his impurity,
and tendered, like Dante his song to the ' ingegni
storti e loschi,' at least an incorruptible beauty :

' Ponete mente *almen* com'io son bella.'

And he understands the meaning of Baudelaire's
definition of reality as ' the adequate union of subject
and object,' and more clearly than ever the grotesque
fallacy of a realistic art—' that miserable statement
of line and surface,' and the penny-a-line vulgarity of
a literature of notations.

He leaves the library and is confronted by the
spectacle of Time made flesh. And whereas a moment ago the bright cymbals of two distant hours,

paralysed at arm's length by the rigid spread of intervening years, had obeyed an irresistible impulse of mutual attraction, and clashed, like storm clouds, in a flash and a brazen peal, now the measure of their span from tip to tip is written on the face and frailty of the dying, curved, like Dante's proud, under the load of their years—' unwieldy, slow, heavy and pale as lead.'

> ' e qual più pazienza avea negli atti
> piangendo parea dicer :—Più non posso.'

We say farewell to M. de Charlus, the Baron Palamède de Charlus, Duke of Brabant, Squire of Montargis, Prince of Oléron, Carency, Viareggio and the Dunes, the unspeakably insolent Charlus, now a humble and convulsive Lear, crowned by the silver torrent of his hair, Oedipus, senile and annulled, stooped over a missal or scraping and bowing before the astonishment of Mme. de Sainte-Euverte, scorned in the full strength of his terrible pride as the Duchesse de Caca or the Princesse de Pipi, the Archangel Raphael in his latter days, still furtively pursuing all the sons of Toby, escorted by the faithful Jupien, Lord of the Temple of Shamelessness. And the dirge of his sepulchral whisper falls like clay from the spade of a gravedigger. ' Hannibal de Bréauté—dead ! Antoine de Mouchy—dead ! Charles Swann—dead ! Adalbert de Montmorency—dead ! Baron de Talleyrand—dead ! Sosthène de Doudeauville—dead ! '

The narrator accomplishes a series of identifications, of voluntary and arduous identifications—balancing those of the library, involuntary and spontaneous. From one sniggering and abject puppet, something between a beggarly hawker and a moribund buffoon, he elicits his enemy, M. d'Argencourt, as he knew him, starched and haughty and impeccable : from a stout dowager, whom he takes at first for Mme. de Forcheville, Gilberte herself. So they drift past, Oriane and the Duc de Guermantes, Rachel and Bloch, Legrandin and Odette, and many others, carrying the burden of Saturn towards the light that will rise, towards Uranus, the Sabbath star.

* *

*

In Time creative and destructive Proust discovers himself as an artist : ' I understood the meaning of death, of love and vocation, of the joys of the spirit and the utility of pain.' Allusion has been made to his contempt for the literature that ' describes,' for the realists and naturalists worshipping the offal of experience, prostrate before the epidermis and the swift epilepsy, and content to transcribe the surface, the façade, behind which the Idea is prisoner. Whereas the Proustian procedure is that of Apollo flaying Marsyas and capturing without sentiment the essence, the Phrygian waters. ' Chi non ha la forza di uccidere la realtà non ha la forza di crearla.' But Proust is too much of an affectivist to be satisfied by the intellectual symbolism of a Baudelaire, abstract and discursive. The Baudelarian unity is a unity 'post rem,' a unity abstracted from plurality. His 'correspondence' is determined by a concept, therefore strictly limited and exhausted by its own definition. Proust does not deal in concepts, he pursues the Idea, the concrete. He admires the frescoes of the Paduan Arena because their symbolism is handled as a reality, special, literal and concrete, and is not merely the pictorial transmission of a notion. Dante, if he can ever be said to have failed, fails with his purely allegorical figures, Lucifer, the Griffin of the Purgatory and the Eagle of the Paradise, whose significance is purely conventional and extrinsic. Here allegory fails as it must always fail in the hands of a poet. Spenser's allegory collapses after a few cantos. Dante, because he was an artist and not a minor prophet, could not prevent his allegory from becoming heated and electrified into anagogy. The *Vision of Mirza* is good allegory because it is flat writing. For Proust the object may be a living symbol, but a symbol of itself. The symbolism of Baudelaire has become the *autosymbolism* of Proust. Proust's point of departure might be situated in Symbolism, or on its outskirts. But he does not proceed pari passu with France, towards an elegant scepticism and the marmorean modes, nor, as we have seen, with Daudet and the Goncourts to the 'notes d'après nature,' nor, of course, with the Parnassians to the ineffable gutter-snippets of François Coppée. He solicits no facts, and he chisels no Cellinesque pommels. He reacts, but in a different direction. He recedes from the Symbolists—back towards Hugo. And for that reason he is a solitary and independent figure. The only contemporary in whom I can discern something of the same retrogressive tendency is Joris Karl Huysmans. But he loathed it in himself and repressed it. He speaks bitterly of the 'ineluctable gangrene of Romanticism,' and yet his des Esseintes is a fabulous creature, an Alfred Lord Baudelaire.

We are frequently reminded of this romantic strain in Proust. He is romantic in his substitution of affectivity for intelligence, in his opposition of the particular affective evidential state to all the subtleties of rational cross-reference, in his rejection of the Concept in favour of the Idea, in his scepticism before causality. Thus his purely logical—as opposed to his intuitive—explanations of a certain effect invariably bristle with alternatives.[1] He is a Romantic in his anxiety to accomplish his mission, to be a good and faithful servant. He does not seek to evade the im-

[1] Cp. for this anti-intellectual tendency: *Swann*, i. 286, ii. 29 and 234; *Guermantes*, i. 162 (Saint-Loup's gesture ex nihilo); *Albertine Disparue*, i. 14 and *passim*.

plications of his art such as it has been revealed to him. He will write as he has lived—in Time. The classical artist assumes omniscience and omnipotence. He raises himself artificially out of Time in order to give relief to his chronology and causality to his development. Proust's chronology is extremely difficult to follow, the succession of events spasmodic, and his characters and themes, although they seem to obey an almost insane inward necessity, are presented and developed with a fine Dostoievskian contempt for the vulgarity of a plausible concatenation. (Proust's impressionism will bring us back to Dostoievski.) Generally speaking, the romantic artist is very much concerned with Time and aware of the importance of memory in inspiration,

('c'est toi qui dors dans l'ombre,
ô sacré souvenir ! . . .)

but is inclined to sensationalise what is treated by Proust with pathological power and sobriety. With Musset, for example, the interest is more in a vague extratemporal identification, without any real cohesion or simultaneity, between the me and not-me than in the functional evocations of a specialised memory. But the analogy is too blurred and would lead nowhere, although Proust quotes Chateaubriand and Amiel as his spiritual ancestors. It is difficult to connect Proust with this pair of melancholy Pantheists dancing a fandango of death in the twilight.

But Proust admired the poetry of the Comtesse de Noailles. Saperlipopette !

The narrator had ascribed his ' lack of talent ' to a lack of observation, or rather to what he supposed was a non-artistic habit of observation. He was incapable of recording surface. So that when he reads such brilliant crowded reporting as the Goncourts' Journal, the only alternative to the conclusion that he is entirely wanting in the precious journalistic talent is the supposition that between the banality of life and the magic of literature there is a great gulf fixed. Either he is devoid of talent or art of reality. And he describes the radiographical quality of his observation. The copiable he does not see. He searches for a relation, a common factor, substrata. Thus he is less interested in what is said than in the way in which it is said. Similarly his faculties are more violently activated by intermediate than by terminal—capital—stimuli. We find countless examples of these secondary reflexes. Withdrawn in his cool dark room at Combray he extracts the total essence of a scorching midday from the scarlet stellar blows of a hammer in the street and the chamber-music of flies in the gloom. Lying in bed at dawn, the exact quality of the weather, temperature and visibility, is transmitted to him in terms of sound, in the chimes and the calls of the hawkers. Thus can be explained the primacy of instinctive perception—intuition—in the

Proustian world. Because instinct, when not vitiated by Habit, is also a reflex, from the Proustian point of view ideally remote and indirect, a chain-reflex. Now he sees his regretted failure to observe artistically as a series of 'inspired omissions' and the work of art as neither created nor chosen, but discovered, un-covered, excavated, pre-existing within the artist, a law of his nature. The only reality is provided by the hieroglyphics traced by inspired perception (identification of subject and object). The conclusions of the intelligence are merely of arbitrary value, potentially valid. 'An impression is for the writer what an experiment is for the scientist—with this difference, that in the case of the scientist the action of the intelligence precedes the event and in the case of the writer follows it.' Consequently for the artist, the only possible hierarchy in the world of objective phenomena is represented by a table of their respective coefficients of penetration, that is to say, in terms of the subject. (Another sneer at the realists.) The artist has acquired his text : the artisan translates it. 'The duty and the task of a writer (not an artist, a writer) are those of a translator.' The reality of a cloud reflected in the Vivonne is not expressed by 'Zut alors' but by the interpretation of that inspired criticism. The verbal oblique must be restored to the upright : thus 'you are charming' equals 'it gives me pleasure to embrace you.'

Proust's relativism and impressionism are adjuncts of this same anti-intellectual attitude. Curtius speaks of Proust's ' perspectivism ' and ' positive relativism ' as opposed to the negative relativism of the late nineteenth century, the scepticism of Renan and France. I think the phrase ' positive relativism ' is an oxymoron, I am almost sure that it does not apply to Proust, and I know that it came out of the Heidelberg laboratory. We have seen how in the case of Albertine (and Proust extends his experience to all human relations) the multiple aspects (read Blickpunkt for this miserable word) did not bind into any positive synthesis. The object evolves, and by the time the conclusion—if any—is reached, it is already out of date. In a sense Proust is a positivist, but his positivism has nothing to do with his relativism, which is as pessimistic and as negative as that of France, and employed as an element of comedy. The ' book,' for Proust a literary statement, is for the housekeeper a book of accounts and for Her Highness the visitors' register. Rachel Quand du Seigneur represents for the narrator thirty francs and a bored satisfaction, for Saint-Loup a fortune and unending misery. Similarly when Saint-Loup sees Albertine's photograph he cannot conceal his astonishment that such a vulgar nonentity should have attracted his brilliant and popular friend. The Comte de Crécy carves a turkey and establishes a calendar as surely as the death of Christ or the departure out of Egypt. For the Baron Musset's ' infidèle ' must be a buttons or a bus-conductor. This relativism is negative and comic. He owes his exaltation on hearing Vinteuil's music to the actress Léa, who alone could decipher the composer's posthumous manuscripts, and to the relations of Charlus with Charlie Morel, the violinist. Proust is positive only in so far as he affirms the value of intuition.

By his impressionism I mean his non-logical statement of phenomena in the order and exactitude of their perception, before they have been distorted into intelligibility in order to be forced into a chain of cause and effect.[1] The painter Elstir is the type of the impressionist, stating what he sees and not what he knows he ought to see : for example, applying urban terms to the sea and marine terms to the town, so as to transmit his intuition of their homogeneity. And we are reminded of Schopenhauer's definition of the artistic procedure as ' the contemplation of the world independently of the principle of reason.' In this connection Proust can be related to Dostoievski, who states his characters without explaining them. It may be objected that Proust does little else but

---

[1] Examples : a napkin in the dust taken for a pencil of light, the sound of water in the pipes for a dog barking or the hooting of a siren, the noise of a spring-door closing for the orchestration of the Pilgrims' Chorus.

explain his characters. But his explanations are experimental and not demonstrative. He explains them in order that they may appear as they are—inexplicable. He explains them away.[1]

Proust's style was generally resented in French literary circles. But now that he is no longer read, it is generously conceded that he might have written an even worse prose than he did. At the same time, it is difficult to estimate with justice a style of which one can only take cognisance by a process of deduction, in an edition that cannot be said to have transmitted the writings of Proust, but to have betrayed a tendency in that direction. For Proust, as for the painter, style is more a question of vision than of technique. Proust does not share the superstition that form is nothing and content everything, nor that the ideal literary masterpiece could only be communicated in a series of absolute and monosyllabic propositions. For Proust the quality of language is more important than any system of ethics or aesthetics. Indeed he makes no attempt to dissociate form from content. The one is a concretion of the other, the revelation of a world. The Proustian world is expressed metaphorically by the artisan because it is apprehended metaphorically by the artist : the indirect and comparative expression of indirect and

[1] Cp. analogy between Dostoievski and Mme. de Sévigné : *A l'Ombre des Jeunes Filles en Fleurs*, ii. 75.

comparative perception. The rhetorical equivalent of the Proustian real is the chain-figure of the metaphor. It is a tiring style, but it does not tire the mind. The clarity of the phrase is cumulative and explosive. One's fatigue is a fatigue of the heart, a blood fatigue. One is exhausted and angry after an hour, submerged, dominated by the crest and break of metaphor after metaphor : but never stupefied. The complaint that it is an involved style, full of periphrasis, obscure and impossible to follow, has no foundation whatsoever.

It is significant that the majority of his images are botanical. He assimilates the human to the vegetal. He is conscious of humanity as flora, never as fauna. (There are no black cats and faithful hounds in Proust.) He deplores ' the time one wastes in upholstering one's life with a human and parasitic vegetation.' The wife and son of the Sidaner amateur appear to him on the shore at Balbec as two flowering ranunculi. Albertine's laugh has the colour and smell of a geranium. Gilberte and Odette are lilacs, white and violet. He speaks of a scene in *Pelléas et Mélisande* that exasperates his rose-fever and makes him sneeze. This preoccupation accompanies very naturally his complete indifference to moral values and human justices.[1] Flower and plant have no conscious will. They are shameless, exposing their

[1] Cp. *La Prisonnière*, ii. 119.

genitals. And so in a sense are Proust's men and women, whose will is blind and hard, but never self-conscious, never abolished in the pure perception of a pure subject. They are victims of their volition, active with a grotesque predetermined activity, within the narrow limits of an impure world. But shameless. There is no question of right and wrong. Homosexuality is never called a vice : it is as devoid of moral implications as the mode of fecundation of the *Primula veris* or the *Lythrum salicoria*. And, like members of the vegetable world, they seem to solicit a pure subject, so that they may pass from a state of blind will to a state of representation. Proust is that pure subject. He is almost exempt from the impurity of will.[1] He deplores his lack of will until he understands that will, being utilitarian, a servant of intelligence and habit, is not a condition of the artistic experience. When the subject is exempt from will the object is exempt from causality (Time and Space taken together). And this human vegetation is purified in the transcendental aperception that can capture the Model, the Idea, the Thing in itself.

So that there is no collapse of the will in Proust, as there is for example in Spenser and Keats and Giorgione. He sits up all night in Paris, with a

[1] Cp. *Swann*, i. 22, 24, 59 and *passim*; *Guermantes*, i. 63; *Sodome et Gomorrhe*, ii. 2, 188; *Albertine Disparue*, ii. 149 (Paralysed by 'O Sole Mio' in Venice).

branch of apple-blossom laid beside his lamp, staring at the foam of the white corollae until the dawn comes to redden them. But this is not the terrible panic-stricken stasis of Keats, crouched in a mossy thicket, annulled, like a bee, in sweetness, ' drowsed with the fume of poppies ' and watching ' the last oozings, hours by hours ' ; nor yet the remote, still, almost breathless passion of a Giorgione youth, the spirit shattered in corruption, damp and rotting, so finely suggested by d'Annunzio in his description of the Concerto (' ma se io penso alle sue mani nascoste, le immagino nell'atto di frangere le foglie del lauro per profumarsene le dita ') and so grossly misinterpreted by the same writer when he sees in the rapt doomed figure of the Tempesta a vulgar Leander resting between orgasms ; nor yet the horrible pomegranates of ' Il Fuoco,' bursting and bleeding, dripping the red ooze of their seed, putrid on the putrid water. The Proustian stasis is contemplative, a pure act of under-standing, will-less, the ' amabilis insania ' and the ' hölder Wahnsinn.'

A book could be written on the significance of music in the work of Proust, in particular of the music of Vinteuil : the Sonata and the Septuor. The influ-ence of Schopenhauer on this aspect of the Proustian demonstration is unquestionable. Schopenhauer re-jects the Leibnitzian view of music as ' occult arith-metic,' and in his aesthetics separates it from the

other arts, which can only produce the Idea with its
concomitant phenomena, whereas music is the Idea
itself, unaware of the world of phenomena, existing
ideally outside the universe, apprehended not in
Space but in Time only, and consequently untouched
by the teleological hypothesis. This essential quality
of music is distorted by the listener who, being an
impure subject, insists on giving a figure to that which
is ideal and invisible, on incarnating the Idea in what
he conceives to be an appropriate paradigm. Thus,
by definition, opera is a hideous corruption of this
most immaterial of all the arts : the words of a
libretto are to the musical phrase that they particu-
larise what the Vendôme Column, for example, is to
the ideal perpendicular. From this point of view
opera is less complete than vaudeville, which at least
inaugurates the comedy of an exhaustive enumera-
tion. These considerations explain the beautiful convention of the ' da capo ' as a testimony to the
intimate and ineffable nature of an art that is perfectly intelligible and perfectly inexplicable. Music
is the catalytic element in the work of Proust. It
asserts to his unbelief the permanence of personality
and the reality of art. It synthesises the moments of
privilege and runs parallel to them. In one passage
he describes the recurrent mystical experience as ' a
purely musical impression, non-extensive, entirely
original, irreducible to any other order of impres-

71

sion, . . . sine materia.' The narrator—unlike Swann who identifies the ' little phrase ' of the Sonata with Odette, spatialises what is extraspatial, establishes it as the national anthem of his love—sees in the red phrase of the Septuor, trumpeting its victory in the last movement like a Mantegna archangel clothed in scarlet, the ideal and immaterial statement of the essence of a unique beauty, a unique world, the invariable world and beauty of Vinteuil, expressed timidly, as a prayer, in the Sonata, imploringly, as an aspiration, in the Septuor, the ' invisible reality ' that damns the life of the body on earth as a pensum and reveals the meaning of the word : ' defunctus.'

EVERGREEN BOOKS

Other Titles In Preparation

PUBLISHED BY

GROVE PRESS, 795 Broadway, New York 3, N. Y.